Selected from

The Best of

Dear Abby

Abigail
Van Buren

WRITERS' VOICES

SIGNAL HILL

WRITERS' VOICES ™ was made possible by grants from: An anonymous foundation; The Vincent Astor Foundation; Booth Ferris Foundation; Exxon Corporation; James Money Management, Inc.; Knight Foundation; Philip Morris Companies Inc.; Scripps Howard Foundation; The House of Seagram; and the H.W. Wilson Foundation.

• • •

ATTENTION READERS: We would like to hear what you think about our books. Please send your comments or suggestions to:

The Editors
New Readers Press
P.O. Box 131
Syracuse, NY 13210-0131

• • •

Selection: From THE BEST OF DEAR ABBY by Abigail Van Buren. © 1981, 1989 by Phillips-Van Buren. Reprinted with permission of Andrews & McMeel. All rights reserved.

SIGNAL HILL

Additional material
© 1991 Signal Hill Publications
A publishing imprint of Laubach Literacy International

10 9 8 7 6 5 4 3 2

ISBN 1-929631-25-0

First printing: March 1991

The words "Writers' Voices" are a trademark of New Readers Press.

Cover designed by Paul Davis Studio
Interior designed by Paolo Pepe

 PRINTED WITH SOY INK ™

 This book was printed on 100% recycled paper which contains 50% post-consumer waste.

Acknowledgments

We gratefully acknowledge the generous support of the following foundations and corporations that made the publication of WRITERS' VOICES and NEW WRITERS' VOICES possible: An anonymous foundation; The Vincent Astor Foundation; Booth Ferris Foundation; Exxon Corporation; James Money Management, Inc.; Knight Foundation; Philip Morris Companies Inc.; Scripps Howard Foundation; The House of Seagram; and the H.W. Wilson Foundation.

This book could not have been realized without the kind and generous cooperation of the author, Abigail Van Buren, and her publisher, Andrews & McMeel. Thanks also to John P. McMeel.

We deeply appreciate the contributions of the following suppliers: Cam Steel Die Rule Works Inc. (steel cutting die for display); Canadian Pacific Forest Products Ltd. (text stock); ComCom (text typesetting); Horizon Paper Co., Inc. and Domtar Fine Papers (cover stock); MCUSA (display header); Delta Corrugated Container (corrugated display); Phototype Color Graphics (cover color separations); and Arcata Graphics Company/Buffalo (cover and text printing and binding).

Our thanks to Paul Davis Studio and Myrna Davis, Paul Davis, Jeanine Esposito, Alex Ginns and Frank Begrowicz for their inspired design of the covers of these books. Thanks also to Paolo Pepe for his sensitive design of the interior of this book, Karen Bernath for design of maps and diagrams, and Ron Bel Bruno for his timely help.

CONTENTS

Note to the Reader

The Best of Dear Abby is about the famous "Dear Abby" newspaper advice column. It contains a special kind of writing—letters. Most letters are fun to get and read. But many people find letters hard to write. Reading this book can help you see different ways people tell about themselves through letters.

Every writer has a special voice. That is why we call our series *Writers' Voices*. We chose *The Best of Dear Abby* because Abby's voice and the voices of the ordinary and not so ordinary people who write to Abby can be clearly heard. In choosing parts from the book, we thought you might like to know a little about Abby's life and to read about the different problems she's tried to help people with.

Reading "About the Selections from *The Best of Dear Abby*" on page 10 will help you begin thinking about what you will read in the selections.

In addition to selections from *The Best of Dear Abby*, this book includes chapters with interesting and helpful information related to the selections. You may read these before or after reading the selections. You may choose to read some or all of these chapters.

- If you would like more information about the history of newspaper advice columns, look at the chapter called "About Advice Columns" on page 51.
- If you would like more information about how newspaper columns are bought and sold, look at the chapter called "About Newspapers and Syndication" on page 53.
- If you would like more information about how to write your own letters, look at the chapter called "About Writing Letters" on page 55.

If you are a new reader, you may want to have this book read aloud to you, perhaps more than once. Even if you are a more experienced reader, you may enjoy hearing it read aloud before reading it silently to yourself.

We encourage you to read *actively*. Here are some things you can do.

BEFORE READING
- Read the front and back covers of the book, and look at the cover illustration. Ask yourself what you expect the book to be about.
- Think about why you want to read this book. Perhaps you have heard of the "Dear Abby" column and want to know more about Abby.

Perhaps you enjoy reading letters. Perhaps you think you might get some good advice from other people's experiences.

• Look at the Contents page. See where you can find a list of some of the newspapers that carry "Dear Abby" and other information. Decide what you want to read and in what order.

DURING READING

• There may be names or other words that are difficult to read. Keep reading to see if the meaning becomes clear. If it doesn't, go back and reread the difficult part or discuss it with others. Or look up the words in the dictionary.

• Ask yourself questions as you read. For example: Do I agree with Abby's answers to people's letters?

AFTER READING

• Think about what you have read. Did you identify with Abby and with some of the people writing to her? Did reading a letter change your thinking about different ways to solve a problem?

• Talk with others about your thoughts.

• Try some of the questions and activities in "Questions for the Reader" on page 47. They are meant to help you discover more about what you have read and how it relates to you.

The editors of *Writers' Voices* hope you will write to us. We want to know your thoughts about our books.

About the Selections from
The Best of Dear Abby

The Best of Dear Abby contains letters and answers from the famous "Dear Abby" newspaper advice column.

The first part of the selection is a long letter from Abby to her readers. In it, Abby tells about her life and how she became "Dear Abby." Abby is short for Abigail Van Buren, a name she made up for her column. Her real name is Pauline Esther Friedman Phillips. She also mentions her famous twin sister who writes the "Ann Landers" advice column.

The rest of the selection is made up of some of the letters that were written to Abby by readers of her column over the last 35 years. Most letters are followed by Abby's reply.

The "Dear Abby" column has been in newspapers since 1955. More people read the "Dear Abby" column than any advice column in the world. It runs in more than 1,200 newspapers in the United States and other countries.

Abby receives as many as 12,000 letters every week. All kinds of people write to her. They may be young or old, rich or poor, female or male. They write for advice about personal problems. Over the years, many of these problems have had to do with marriage, children and in-laws. Other problems, such as those about teenage sex and pregnancy, homosexuality, drug abuse and AIDS, are new to the column.

Abby, or Abigail Van Buren, has seen other changes in the letters people have written to her over the years. In the past, most of the letters were from women. Now nearly half of them are from men. She also says that people are more open in writing about their problems now than they were 35 years ago.

Abby has changed the way she feels about some of the problems she writes about. One of the most important changes is her attitude toward marriage. When she began, Abby told couples to stay together "for the sake of the marriage," even if they were having problems. She thought this would keep the family together. Now she believes that if a marriage is really in trouble, the couple should separate. She has come to think that keeping a bad marriage together will not solve the problem. It will only make everyone unhappy, especially the children.

One thing has not changed. Whatever subject people write to her about, Abby treats it seriously. She knows that people write to her because they need to "unload, confess, or sound off." And they expect Abby to "listen without sitting in judgment."

In the second part of this selection, you will find letters on many subjects. They include marriage, divorce, cheating on a spouse, "other women," premarital sex, love between older adults, lack of interest in sex, jealousy, disciplining children, teenagers, homosexuality, pets, house guests, birth defects and New Year's resolutions.

Most people who write to Abby sign their letters with their complete names and addresses, in case Abby wants to write to them directly. Others just use their first names or a *pseudonym*. Pseudonyms are names people have made up for themselves. Using only a first name or a pseudonym can make a writer feel freer about discussing his or her private problems. But Abby protects the privacy of everyone who writes to her by making up a name for each letter writer who appears in her column.

The pseudonyms Abby or writers choose usually tell something about the kind of problem the person is writing about and how they feel about it. A letter signed "Alone and Crying" is from a woman who writes about the man who left her. A mother who signs "Ashamed to

Sign My Name" writes about her teenage daughter using birth control.

Maybe reading these letters will help you to solve a problem that has troubled you. Or it may lead you to write a letter to "Dear Abby" to tell Abby about your problem or to offer different advice from what she has given someone else.

MAP OF PLACES MENTIONED IN THE SELECTIONS

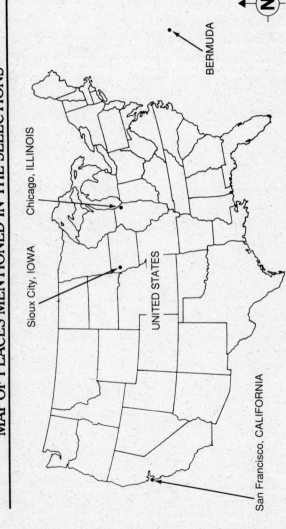

Selected from
The Best of Dear Abby
Abigail Van Buren

———————●———————

DEAR READERS

Some thirty-three years ago, I, Pauline Esther Phillips, conceived and gave birth to Abigail Van Buren—better known as Dear Abby.

But let's start at the beginning:

When I came into the world on July 4, 1918, in Sioux City, Iowa, I was named Pauline Esther Friedman. My identical twin sister, who had made her debut just seventeen minutes earlier, had been named Esther Pauline. From that day on we were known as "the Friedman Twins."

As soon as we were old enough to talk, my twin called me "Popo" and I called her "Eppie." Friends who knew us B.C. (Before Column) still use those names, although the world has since come to know us as "Dear Abby" and "Ann Landers."

From my earliest recollections we were a team. We looked alike, talked alike, thought alike, and Mama always dressed us alike. We were precocious, mischievous, talkative, extroverted and cute. We were also creative. As children we were constantly collaborating on poems, parodies, and witty letters.

We twins were the youngest of four daughters and the only two who pursued professional careers.

After graduating from high school my twin sister and I enrolled at Morningside, the local college. We had dreams of going to Northwestern University but were told we couldn't afford it. That may have been true, but our two older sisters had married and left home, and I suspect our parents wanted to keep their youngest around as long as possible.

Because we enjoyed writing, we signed up for the journalism course in our freshman year. We immediately started writing for the college weekly, and together we originated a lively little gossip column which we named "The Campus Rat."

We also took courses in philosophy, biology, English literature, and theology, but the only degrees we hold today are honorary, because we dropped out during our junior year to marry.

On July 2, 1939 (just two days before their twenty-first birthday), the Friedman Twins co-starred in a spectacular double-feature wedding.

It was a production the likes of which Sioux City had never seen before—or since.

There was standing-room only in the flower-filled synagogue where friends and relatives had come to see a very proud father walk down the aisle with a twin bride on each arm.

I married Morton Phillips, a student at the University of Minnesota, who lacked a month of being twenty-one.

In 1955 Mort bought a business in San Francisco and we headed for California. When we moved west, Eppie and her husband moved to Chicago.

Eppie phoned with some exciting news. A friend of hers who was an executive with the *Chicago Sun-Times* newspaper syndicate had called to tell her that Ruth Crowley, the woman who had been writing the syndicate-owned Ann Landers column, had died suddenly and they needed a replacement. Was Eppie interested in competing for the job?

Was she ever! (At that time, the Ann Landers column had a comparatively modest syndication, which has increased impressively since Eppie took over.)

For the first few months Eppie sent me batches of letters from readers, and I'd shoot back my suggested replies. Many were used, and I became fascinated with the opportunity to do something creative, entertaining, and helpful. I was ecstatically happy and having a ball!

Then, suddenly, the ball was over. Eppie called to say that her syndicate had put the kibosh on her sending mail "outside the office," so there would be no more letters coming my way.

Having acquired a taste for dispensing advice, and confident that I could do it well, I pondered the possibilities of writing an advice column locally.

I began to think about the advice column I had been reading every morning in the *San Francisco Chronicle*. The more I thought about it, the more convinced I became that I could do a better job, so I impulsively rang up the *Chronicle* and asked for the feature editor.

Much to my surprise I was put through immediately to one Stanleigh Arnold.

Identifying myself as a Hillsborough housewife, I asked if he would see me for five minutes so I could present an "interesting proposition."

"What about?" he snapped.

"About that advice column you're running," I snapped back. "It's pretty grim."

"And I suppose *you* can write a better one,"

said the short-fused editor. "Fall in line. A lot of people tell me that."

"Then maybe it's time you listened," was my brash reply.

"Well," said Arnold, trying to terminate the conversation as courteously as possible, "if you're ever in the neighborhood, come in and see me." (End of conversation.)

The next morning I headed for the city.

"What newspapers have you written for?" he asked.

I told him that although I had never written professionally, I had taken all the journalism and psychology that my little college back in Sioux City had to offer. Then I recited the long list of volunteer organizations for which I had worked. He was visibly underwhelmed.

Just to get rid of me, he loaded my arms with old copies of the *Chronicle*, told me to substitute my answers to letters that had appeared in the advice column, and come back—in about a week.

I went directly to my husband's office not far from the *Chronicle*, commandeered a typewriter, and whacked out my answers. They were mostly flip, saucy one-liners.

Two hours later I was back at the *Chronicle*. A secretary asked me to leave my work (together with my name and phone number). I was given the old "Don't call us—we'll call you" treatment.

The drive from San Francisco to my home took less than an hour. As I opened my door, the phone was ringing. It was Mr. Arnold. The brass at the *Chronicle* was interested in seeing me again.

That evening I told my husband about the column I might be writing for the *Chronicle*. Then he gave me the most valuable business advice I've ever had: "If you plan to write professionally, copyright your pen name and own it yourself."

The name, of course, was Abigail Van Buren. I took the "Abigail" from the Old Testament, for Abigail was a prophetess in the Book of Samuel, and it was said of her, "Blessed are thou, and blessed is thy advice, O Abigail." For my last name I chose "Van Buren" from our eighth president Martin Van Buren, because I liked the aristocratic, old-family ring.

The column was named "Dear Abby."

I immediately called my twin in Chicago to tell her that I had been hired to write the advice column for the *San Francisco Chronicle*. She said, "Congratulations, that's marvelous. I'm so happy for you!" And I knew she meant it.

So on January 9, 1956, I was launched in my writing career.

"Dear Abby" had been in print only a few months when the publisher of the *New York Mirror* called to say he had seen my column in the *Chronicle* and wanted it for his newspaper as soon as he could get it!

Having no agent or business manager (I still haven't), I discussed the *New York Mirror* offer with my husband. He saw no reason why "Dear Abby" shouldn't appear in the *New York Mirror*. I certainly wasn't competing with my twin, because her column did not run in New York City.

Knowing less than nothing about "syndicates" and how they operated, I sought advice from my bosses at the *San Francisco Chronicle*. They recommended that I sign with "McNaught," a New York syndicate whose representatives just happened to be in town at the moment.

My exposure in New York created a minor sensation, and soon I was getting letters from editors around the country asking *me* how they could get my column.

"Dear Abby" was heralded as "a phenomenon in modern journalism—the fastest rising star in the business."

My career shot upward to undreamed-of

heights, and "Dear Abby" was soon being read by more people in more languages than any other newspaper column in the history of journalism.

Meanwhile back in Chicago, the Ann Landers list of newspapers was growing proportionately, because nearly every city had two newspapers, and when Abby went into one Ann went into the other. The Chicago Sun-Times Syndicate looked upon "Dear Abby" as formidable competition, and they blamed Ann for introducing her twin sister to the lovelorn field.

My twin felt betrayed because I became syndicated. I insisted that the world was big enough for two good advice columns and tried desperately to make her see it my way. I wasn't getting through to her.

Contrary to reports, there never was a time when my twin and I were "not speaking," but I must admit that our once close and loving relationship was badly damaged.

For seven years my career flourished, but I walked around with a hole in my heart. There wasn't a day that I didn't miss my twin and I wrote countless letters telling her so. I even sent her an olive branch once, but she remained distant. As time went by, a reconciliation seemed hopeless.

Then suddenly, on May 4, 1964, my telephone rang, and then I heard that husky voice so like my own say, "Hello, Popo—This is Eppie." My heart started to pound and my throat closed up. I couldn't talk.

Then she asked, "Do you and Mort have any plans for your twenty-fifth wedding anniversary?" (It was hers, too, since we were married together.)

When I finally found my voice I told her that we had been thinking about going to Bermuda for a few weeks.

"Shall we make it a foursome?" she asked.

It took me all of one second to say, "Yes!"

And thus began the reuniting of a pair of identical twins who together have cornered the largest supermarket confessional in the world.

———————•———————

DEAR ABBY: What has happened to you? You used to encourage married couples to do everything within their power to save their marriages. Lately, you give the impression that divorce could be the answer for some couples. Why?

FAITHFUL READER

DEAR READER: Because I think it's more important to save people than marriages. And in some cases, in an effort to save a marriage that isn't worth saving, people have destroyed themselves and each other.

———— • ————

DEAR ABBY: I am absolutely beside myself with the news my parents gave me this morning. They drove over here and calmly announced that after forty-four years of marriage they are getting a divorce! I honestly believe they have taken leave of their senses.

They have had their differences like all married couples, but they have never separated—not even for one day. I can't imagine what has come over them.

Dad says that since he is seventy, if the good Lord gives him another five years he wants to live them in peace. Mother, who is sixty-nine, says she feels the same way.

I suggested a larger apartment with two bedrooms, frequent separate vacations, a trial separation—anything but divorce. But they insist they have thought it over and this is what they both want. Abby, they have children and grandchildren who love and respect them. How can parents disgrace their families that way?

THEIR DAUGHTER

DEAR DAUGHTER: Your parents have a right to make their own decisions, for their own reasons, without loss of love or respect from their children and grandchildren. And if they terminate their marriage after forty-four years, where is the "disgrace"? Perhaps they stayed together as long as they did out of consideration for you. They need compassion, not criticism.

———————•———————

DEAR ABBY: I am married to a man I love with all my heart. He says he no longer loves me and he wants a divorce. We have three children. At first he said there was no one else and he just wanted to be free, then after I begged him to reconsider, he admitted there was another woman.

I would get down on my hands and knees if I thought it would do any good. I tried to tell him how much I loved him. I even kissed him, but he stood there like a statue with his hands in his pockets. Abby, I am desperate. How can I get him to love me again? The divorce is coming up soon in court. No fault. No chance. Help me. I don't want to live without him.

ALONE AND CRYING

DEAR ALONE: You aren't alone. You have three children, which are three good reasons for living.

Since there is another woman in the picture, your chances for making him "love you" again are zilch. Furthermore, there is nothing less appealing to a man than a begging, prideless woman. So dry your tears, square your shoulders, and chin up. Concentrate on making a new life for yourself. Sometimes good luck comes disguised as disaster.

———————●———————

DEAR ABBY: I heard about teen-age rebellion, but I never experienced it until suddenly Joe, seventeen, and Betsy, fifteen, let me know they were "old enough to do as they pleased." Life became one constant battle about hair, clothes, late hours, and poor grades. Taking away privileges and cutting allowances didn't faze them. After I was told for the fiftieth time that they were old enough to do as they pleased, I saw the light.

I told them that by their reasoning I was also "old enough to do as I pleased." Then I sat down with a book, put my feet up, and relaxed. When they asked when dinner would be ready, I told them that whenever it pleased them they could make their own dinner. I then made myself a salad and a hamburger and continued to read my book, ignoring them.

For five days I neither cooked, cleaned, washed nor ironed for them. Only for myself. When they asked me what was wrong with me, I told them I was "old enough to do as I pleased" too, and it pleased me to think of no one but myself.

They finally got the point. Life is now restored to normal, and now we all live by the rules in this house. This may not work for everyone, but it worked for me.

REBELLIOUS MOTHER

●

DEAR ABBY: My telephone just rang. It was a doctor telling me that my sixteen-year-old daughter was just in his office asking for birth control pills. Abby, what are these young people doing to us mothers?

I knew she had a steady boyfriend, but I never dreamed they were in need of anything like that. I am heartsick. I tried to raise the girl right. Where have I failed?

ASHAMED TO SIGN MY NAME

DEAR ASHAMED: You haven't failed, and if you tried to raise her right you need not be ashamed. I am not in favor of premarital sex for teen-agers, but once a girl has gone all the way it is unrealistic to think that she will stop simply because she is denied the pill. So then what? She risks becoming pregnant. And if she does, what has the doctor accomplished? He will have been responsible for (a) an unwanted baby, (b) an abortion, or (c) a hasty marriage. Which would you choose for your daughter?

If you are among those mothers who say, "If that's the way she is going to act, then let her suffer the consequences," please consider the baby. Don't you think every child should come into this world wanted by its natural mother? I do.

———————•———————

DEAR ABBY: I needed some Scotch tape, so I looked in my son's desk for some and noticed the beginning of a letter my son had written to his girlfriend. It read, "I am only interested in being stoned, spending money, and sex."

I read no further.

My first impulse was to confront him with this, but he would say I had no right to go snooping through his desk.

I don't think I should go on ignoring this. I would appreciate some advice. He is eighteen-and-a-half.

BEWILDERED FATHER

DEAR FATHER: You could be about seventeen years too late. It won't help now to be reminded that you failed to build the kind of father-son relationship that inspires trust, confidence, and total honesty. It's possible that what you read did not reflect your son's thoughts accurately, however.

Don't tell him what you saw, but try to get a dialogue going so you can get inside his head. Encourage honesty, and no matter what he says, be cool and don't put him down or make him feel guilty. If you can develop candid two-way communication, you'll be able to influence and eventually help your son. He doesn't need punishment, Father, he needs a mature, understanding friend.

———————•———————

DEAR ABBY: Another advice columnist keeps insisting that homosexuals are "sick." She says, and I quote:

"Thousands of homosexuals have written asking me where they can get 'straightened out,' so they must consider themselves sick—or they wouldn't be asking for help. Occasionally I hear from homosexuals who are at peace with themselves, but they are few and far between.

"I believe the majority of homosexuals

would be straight if they were really free to choose."

What do you say, Dear Abby?

L.A. TIMES READER

DEAR READER: I say if a heterosexual had been raised to believe that his preference for the opposite sex was "sick," twisted, abominable, sinful, and a disgrace to his family, he would ask for help on how to "straighten himself out," too.

Homosexuality is a problem because an unenlightened society has made it a problem, but I have received letters by the thousands (not just "occasionally") from gay people telling me that they wouldn't be straight if they had a choice. All they ask is to be allowed to love in their own way without facing the charge that they are "sick and twisted."

I say, love and let love.

———————•———————

DEAR ABBY: "On the Verge" complained because his wife was frigid.

Abby, you once said, "There are no cold women—only clumsy men." How right you were.

I am a man in my middle fifties. I'm short, balding, and slightly overweight, but I have been with plenty of women, and I have yet to find one that's frigid.

I am not saying this to brag, but once I make love to a woman I can't get rid of her. A woman needs to hear that she's desirable, lovable, and terrific. It's not so much what I *do*, it's what I say. A woman needs to hear that she's needed, wanted, and loved. If a woman is "frigid," it's because the man is selfish, impatient, and doesn't know how to turn her on.

DOING ALL RIGHT

DEAR DOING: You are living proof of what I have long contended. Words are a powerful aphrodisiac. If a woman hears the right things from her lover, he's got it (and her) made.

DEAR ABBY: This morning I was going through my husband's wallet, and I came across a list of ladies' sizes for everything from coats, dresses, gloves, and hosiery to bras. It was "signed" with a lipstick imprint, "From your Honey." What does this mean?

ARLINGTON

DEAR ARLINGTON: It probably means that you can't trust your husband, and somebody else can't trust your husband's memory. (At least you know the vital statistics of your competition.)

———————●———————

DEAR ABBY: If a person wants to visit you, and she knows that her dog doesn't get along with your dog, shouldn't she leave her dog home?

Frisky (my dog) and Gertrude (my friend's dog) nearly had a bloody battle once at my place because they hate the sight of each other, so my friend called up and said she was bringing Gertrude over so I should lock up Frisky. Well, I did, but

Frisky knew they were here, and he cried and carried on the whole time.

I told my friend that next time she wants to visit me, she should leave Gertrude home. My friend says that since she is the guest and I am the hostess, I should defer to her wishes. How would you handle this? I really like my friend, but I don't care for her dog.

FRISKY'S MISTRESS

DEAR MISTRESS: The next time your friend wants to get together, tell her to stay home and lock up Gertrude, because you are coming to visit her and you are bringing Frisky.

———————•———————

DEAR ABBY: In a courtship between a woman sixty-five and a man sixty-seven, who should offer the first kiss?

I am a widow and he is a widower and we are getting very close to where I will need to know.

If he should make the first move, should I act coy, or should I respond? Or perhaps

I should make the first move, but I don't want to push for it.

I would like a romantic relationship!

Women used to sit back and let the men make all the overtures, but perhaps women's lib has changed all that. Or has it?

PROPER BUT PUZZLED

DEAR PUZZLED: If you feel like kissing him, go ahead and kiss him. He'll probably meet you halfway and beat you to the finish line.

———————●———————

DEAR ABBY: My husband is retired now, and most of his cronies are either dead or too sick to be any company to him. He used to be quite the "man about town" and I spent many evenings alone and heavy-hearted wondering when he would come home.

Now, do you know what? I can't get him out of the house. I actually have to look for things for him to do. "Go to the grocery store! Go to the drug store! Go to the hardware store!"

I can't stand the sight of him anymore. I get nauseated when I hear his key in the door.

After he reads the morning paper, he starts to follow me around, supervising the cooking, housekeeping, etc.

If I have a friend in for a cup of tea, he moves right in and monopolizes the conversation.

Dear God, I am so sick of him, death would be a welcome release.

WEARY

DEAR WEARY: Yours or his? The quality of a marriage is only as good as the materials used by the builders. The "lumber of life" is caring, sharing, patience, forgiveness, and understanding. One can't expect to spend his twilight years in a cathedral when he's accumulated only enough "lumber" for a shack.

———————⚫———————

DEAR ABBY: I just read the letter from the twenty-eight-year-old mother of four who tacked a poster on her door with "rules" to keep visitors away.

Well, I'm a thirty-eight-year-old mother of six, and I'm amazed that anyone would want that much privacy. We're newcomers who live in the country, and I'm stuck out here with six kids, two dogs, and three cats. I'm so hungry for company, I'm ready to go out on the road and flag down some strangers.

Please print my "poster" in the paper for all to read:

—You may smoke inside, outside, on the roof, or anywhere you wish, just don't burn the house down.

—If you're hungry, help yourself to anything you can find. And if you can't find anything, ask one of the kids. They'll fix you a peanut butter and brown sugar sandwich.

—If you're here around mealtime, grab a chair and join us.

—If you want to stay overnight, bring a sleeping bag and we'll move some clutter from the corner to make room for you.

—Bring your kids. We have so many, a few more won't make any difference.

—We can't lend you any money, but go ahead and ask anyway. It will make us feel good to know we appear that prosperous.

—Tell us your troubles and we'll tell you ours. One of our kids can play the violin for background music, and we can all cry together.

—If you can stand us, we can stand you, so drop in anytime and stay as long as you like. We're people who like people.

MIDGE IN WATSONVILLE, CAL.

DEAR MIDGE: You sound like the kind of person I'd like to know. I'll bet you won't be hungry for company long.

———————————•———————————

DEAR ABBY: I just can't believe that you took the time to write a personal letter. And when you said, "Please write again. I care," I cried.

Abby, why would anyone want to help me straighten out my rotten mixed-up life? I don't deserve it. Five times people saved me from suicide. Sometimes I wish they'd have let me die—it's so hard to keep saying "thank you."

I'm a registered nurse and should be helping people, but instead people are helping me. I feel so guilty.

I have a fantastic new psychiatrist who acts as though he really cares about me. I don't know why anyone would care if I lived or died. I'm not pretty or smart or productive. I'm a burden and a problem to everyone who knows me. But this doctor makes me feel so great.

Is life worth living to feel great for only one hour a week? Help me.

FINISHED AT TWENTY-FOUR

DEAR TWENTY-FOUR: You're far from finished, you're just beginning to realize how precious life is. Every human being who reaches out for help wants it—and deserves it. It's always darkest just before dawn. Hang in there and don't let your doctor (or yourself) down. You can make it if you try. I'm counting on you.

———————•———————

DEAR ABBY: During my childhood I often caught my mother crying. When I was fourteen, she told me, "Never marry a jealous man." I paid little attention. In fact, I gave it no thought until I married one myself.

All the signs were there for me to read, but when you're in love you think your love can conquer all. It can't.

When I married Roy, I was a virgin and he knew it but as far as he was concerned, I could just as well have been a street-walker. After we were married he repeatedly insulted me, saying it was impossible for a pretty girl to have worked alongside men as I have done and remain a virgin. I should have said goodbye right then and there, but I had been raised to believe that "divorce" was a disgrace. Then Roy started to accuse me of every man I had ever known. I thought a "family" would solve everything, so in five years I had two babies.

Nothing changed. For twenty-two years I lived in hell, but I finally won. Both children have college degrees and have grown up to be worthwhile people. I have kept my mouth shut when the mere effort made my jaws ache.

When the youngest was twenty-one and established, I walked out on Roy. Since then, I have put him completely out of my life. I heard recently that he had died. The news (if true) leaves me cold. My "husband" died years ago.

Am I disloyal? I don't think so. I am probably writing this to get it off my chest.

I didn't pay any attention to my mother when she told me not to marry a jealous man. And maybe nobody will pay any attention to me. But when that innocent little girl wrote to you saying, "I'm glad my fiancé is jealous. It just proves he 'loves' me," I wanted to scream!

That poor little thing. Little does she know that it proves nothing of the sort. Jealousy has nothing to do with love. It's a sickness. And no amount of patience, sacrifice, giving in, or giving up will cure it. I know this is too long for your column, but I just had to have my say.

PEACE AT LAST

DEAR PEACE: It's long, all right, but I didn't have the heart to cut it. Some people do learn from the mistakes of others. You've paid the "tuition"—perhaps a reader will read this and get by on a "scholarship."

DEAR ABBY: Please tell me what to do when a friend has had an abnormal child (a Mongoloid)?

I certainly can't send a card or gift of "congratulations" to someone who has had such a tragedy. Would a message of "sympathy" be more in order? Or should something like this be acknowledged at all?

OKLAHOMAN

DEAR OKLAHOMAN: A child, normal or otherwise, is a child to his mother. Don't differentiate. Send a little gift with your love and best wishes.

———•———

DEAR ABBY: I want to say "thank you" for something you did for me.

On May 6, our second son was born. But he was not like our first, healthy, "normal" son. He is Mongoloid. With the help of family, friends, and doctors, I prepared myself for the raising of our "special" child. But the acceptance came much harder for my proud husband. It's easier for a mother to love the child she has carried for nine months, but for the father, that love sometimes comes harder, and after many forced smiles and sleepless nights, my husband now admits that he was miserable. Needlessly miserable, he knows now, but at first he wondered if he could ever "love" his second son as he should.

On May 11, your column concerning Mongoloid babies appeared. It could not have come out at a better time for us. That made the difference in my husband's life. After reading that column, he no longer had that "why-did-this-have-to-happen-to-us" attitude. And just knowing how other people have handled it can help a lot.

Our baby is eight months old now, and a happier child I've never seen. And I know a lot of his happiness comes from knowing that his mother and daddy and brother really love and accept him totally.

Dear, Dear Abby, if you did nothing else this year, you have helped one father find the love he always had for his "special" child. Thank you!

DOUG'S MOTHER

DEAR MOTHER: Your letter made this five-feet-nothing columnist nine feet tall today. After this appears, I know I'll be deluged with requests to reprint the column, so tomorrow, with the kind indulgence of those readers who have already read it, I shall do so.

———————————●———————————

A few years ago I thought it would be appropriate to publish some resolutions on New Year's Day. As I began to write them I recalled something in the Overeaters Anonymous literature that said in essence what I had in mind. I found it, made some revisions and came up with a column that has become a New Year's Day tradition.

1. Just for today I will try to live through this day only, and not set far-reaching goals to try to overcome all my problems at once. I know I can do something for twelve hours that would appall me if I felt that I had to keep it up for a lifetime.

2. Just for today I will try to be happy. Abraham Lincoln said, "Most folks are about as happy as they make up their minds to be." He was right. I will not dwell on thoughts that depress

me. I will chase them out of my mind and replace them with happy thoughts.

3. Just for today I will adjust myself to what is. I will face reality. I will try to change those things which I can change, and accept those things I cannot change.

4. Just for today I will try to improve my mind. I will not be a mental loafer. I will force myself to read something that requires effort, thought, and concentration.

5. Just for today I will exercise my soul in three ways: I will do a good deed for somebody—without letting them know it. (If they find out I did it, it won't count.) I will do at least two things that I know I should do but have been putting off. I will not show anyone that my feelings are hurt; they may be hurt, but today I will not show it.

6. Just for today I will be agreeable. I will look as well as I can, dress becomingly, talk softly, act courteously, and speak ill of no one. Just for today I'll

not try to improve anybody except myself.

7. Just for today I will have a program. I may not follow it exactly, but I will have it, thereby saving myself from two pests: hurry and indecision.

8. Just for today I will have a quiet half hour to relax alone. During this time I will reflect on my behavior and will try to get a better perspective on my life.

9. Just for today I will be unafraid. I will gather the courage to do what is right and take the responsibility for my own actions. I will expect nothing from the world, but I will realize that as I give to the world, the world will give to me.

———————•———————

Questions for
the Reader

THINKING ABOUT THE WRITING

1. What was interesting for you about the selections from *The Best of Dear Abby*? Did you think "Dear Abby" gave helpful advice? Are there letters you would answer differently?

2. Were there ways the letters in the selections became important or special to you? Which letters were the most interesting to you? Write about or discuss these.

3. From her answers to letters, did you get an idea of what kind of person Abigail Van Buren is? How would you describe her? Give some examples from her answers that tell about the kind of person she is.

4. In what ways did the selections answer the questions you had before you began reading or listening?

5. Are there any subjects that you think

"Dear Abby" should *not* write about? Give some examples and tell why.

6. Were any parts of the selections difficult to understand? If so, you may want to read or listen to them again. Discuss with your learning partners possible reasons why they were difficult.

ACTIVITIES

1. Were there any words that were difficult for you in the selections from *The Best of Dear Abby*? Go back to these words and try to figure out their meanings. Discuss what you think each word means, and why you made that guess. Look them up in a dictionary and see if your definitions are the same or different.

Discuss with your learning partners how you are going to remember each word. Some ways to remember words are to put them on file cards, write them in a journal, or create a personal dictionary. Be sure to use the words in your writing in a way that will help you to remember their meaning.

2. Talking with other people about what you have read can increase your understanding. Dis-

cussion can help you organize your thoughts, get new ideas and rethink your original ideas. Discuss your thoughts about the selections with someone else who has read them. Find out if you helped yourself understand the selections in the same or different ways. Find out if your opinions about the selections are the same or different. See if your thoughts change as a result of this discussion.

3. After you finish reading or listening, you might want to write down your thoughts about the book. You could write your reflections on the book in a journal, or you could write about topics the book has brought up that you want to explore further. You could write a book review or a letter to a friend you think might be interested in the book.

4. Did reading the selections give you any ideas for your own writing? You might want to:

• Write a letter about a problem you are having. If you do not want to write about your own problems, describe a problem you know other people have had.

• Write a reply that gives better advice, if you disagree with some of Abby's advice.

• Pretend you are the editor of "Dear Abby." Write a letter to Abby that tells how she could make her column better.

5. Look over the pseudonyms people use when writing their letters. Which ones do you think are the most descriptive? Try making up your own pseudonyms for letters in the book or for your own letters.

6. Would you enjoy writing an advice column? Think about how you would start an advice column in your local or school newspaper. How would your column be similar to or different from "Dear Abby"?

7. Write a letter to the editor of your local newspaper, the mayor, the president or another government official about an issue that concerns you.

About
Advice Columns

The "Dear Abby" column is part of a long tradition of personal advice columns that goes back nearly 100 years. It all began in the Deep South, in New Orleans, Louisiana.

The first regular advice column was called "Dorothy Dix Talks." It appeared in a New Orleans newspaper in 1896 and was written by Dorothy Dix.

Dorothy Dix's real name was Elizabeth Meriwether Gilmer. She wrote the column to support herself and her incurably ill husband.

Like advice columnists today, Dorothy Dix offered simple, down-to-earth suggestions. She was very popular and her column came to be published in over 300 different newspapers.

The kind of advice column that Dorothy Dix wrote and Abby writes was once known as an "advice to the lovelorn" column. The "lovelorn" were people who had been unlucky in love or had been hurt by a loved one.

Advice-to-the-lovelorn columns became very popular over the years. Most newspapers had some kind of advice column. The writers of the columns became well known. Books and movies were even written about advice-to-the-lovelorn columnists. One famous book is *Miss Lonely-hearts* by Nathanael West. It was written in 1933. It is a sad and funny story about the man who writes the "Miss Lonelyhearts" column for a newspaper called the *New York Post-Dispatch*.

As the years passed, lovelorn columns talked about different problems. People asked questions about more than their love lives. They wanted to know about how to handle problems with their families and friends. They asked about problems of society and the world.

Two people who helped to shape the advice column into what it is today are Abigail Van Buren, or "Dear Abby," and Ann Landers. Ann Landers and Abigail Van Buren are twin sisters. Ann Landers' real name is Esther Pauline Friedman Lederer. Abigail Van Buren's real name is Pauline Esther Friedman Phillips.

Ann Landers began her advice column in 1955 for the *Chicago Sun-Times*. Abigail Van Buren began her "Dear Abby" column in 1956 for the *San Francisco Chronicle*. Both have written their columns ever since. They have talked about much more than love. They have written about problems with families and friends and all the other problems that people face.

About Newspapers and Syndication

You may read the "Dear Abby" column in your local newspaper. But your hometown newspaper is not the only place the "Dear Abby" column appears. The column you read will be in hundreds of newspapers across the United States. Sometimes it will even appear in two newspapers in the same city.

This is because the "Dear Abby" column is *syndicated.* A syndicate is a big distribution system. A syndicate owns the rights to put columns like "Dear Abby" in newspapers all over the world.

Big businesses or newspapers own and run syndicates. A syndicate sells advice columns like "Dear Abby," comic strips and opinion columns to newspapers that want to print them.

There are many syndicates in the United States and across the world. The syndicate that distributes "Dear Abby" is Universal Press Syndicate. The comic strip "Calvin and Hobbes" is also distributed by Universal Press Syndicate.

Newspapers That Feature "Dear Abby"

The "Dear Abby" column runs in over 1,200 newspapers around the world. Some of the newspapers in the United States are:

Atlanta Constitution
Boston Herald
Chicago Tribune
Dallas Morning News
Hartford Courant
Kansas City Star
Los Angeles Times
Miami Herald
New York Daily News
New York Newsday
Rocky Mountain News
St. Louis Post-Dispatch
St. Paul Pioneer Press-Dispatch
San Francisco Chronicle
Seattle Times

"Dear Abby" runs in many other newspapers. Look in your local newspapers to find her column.

About
Writing Letters

This book may inspire you to write a letter to "Dear Abby" or to someone else. People write two kinds of letters: *business letters* or *personal letters*.

A *personal letter* goes to a friend or family member. In it, you usually talk about what you are doing and ask about how your friends or family are. You usually write a personal letter by hand.

Some examples of personal letters are:
• a thank-you note for a present or an invitation to an event
• a note of condolence to the family of someone who has died
• letters to friends and family who live far away or are in the service.

Sample personal letter

November 11, 1990

Dear Margaret,

How are you and the family? We are all well. The kids are growing so fast. I hope you can come out and visit us soon. We would love to see you all.

Your loving brother,
Tom

In a personal letter, you usually put the date at the top of the page. Since you are writing to someone you know well, you address her by her first name: "Dear Margaret". After the greeting, a comma (,) is used. The closing is usually something personal: "Your loving brother" or "Affectionately" or "Love." After the closing, a comma (,) is used.

You write a *business letter* to someone you may not know personally, but to whom you have something to say in writing. The person usually works in a business, in government or at a newspaper. You can write a business letter by hand, but it is best to type it.

Some examples of business letters are:

- a letter asking for information or an application (for a driver's license or a job)
- a letter complaining about bad repair work, a delay in delivery or an incorrect bill (to a landlord, a department store or a utility company)
- a letter offering your opinion (to a government representative or a newspaper)

A business letter has a definite form. It is usually typed, although it can be neatly printed or written. The letter has four parts—*heading, opening, body* and *closing.*

Sample business letter

(your address)   123 Main Street
                                  Elm City, CT 00000

        (date)   May 25, 1990

Registry of Motor Vehicles
12 Oak Street   (address of place you are
Elm City, CT 00000   writing)

Dear Sir or Madam: OPENING

Please send me an application for
a Connecticut driver's license. Please
send it to this address: BODY
            Mary Smith
            123 Main Street
            Elm City, CT 00000

Thank you.

Sincerely,   CLOSING

Mary Smith

Mary Smith   (signature)

                      (your name)

In this letter, notice that the *heading* is at the top of the page. It includes your address and the date.

The *opening* comes two lines after the address of the person or company to whom you are writing. It is usually a greeting, like "Dear Mr. ———" or "Dear Ms. ———". After the greeting, a colon (:) is used.

The *body* of the letter is next. It is your message or request. This is the main part of the letter.

The *closing* ends the letter. Usually it is simple. A favorite closing is "Sincerely" followed by your name underneath. Some other closings are "Yours truly" or "Best regards". After the closing, a comma (,) is used.

When you have written or typed your letter, sign it in ink and get the envelope ready. On a business envelope, you need to type or write in two sets of names and addresses—your own and the person you are writing to.

Sample envelope

```
Mary Smith
123 Main Street
Elm City, CT 00000



        Registry of Motor Vehicles
        12 Oak Street
        Elm City, CT 00000
```

Now that you know the form of a business letter and envelope, the only question left is, "What should I write in my letter?" You have already seen the types of letters that people write to "Dear Abby." They may be about a lot of different subjects, but they all have one thing in common. The writers tell their ideas right away. For example, if you look at the letters again, you will see that most people describe their problem in the first few sentences.

You will want to write the same kind of short and direct letter for any kind of business letter. To help you get started, examples of two business letters appear on the next two pages.

Letter complaining about a delay in delivery

456 First Avenue
Springfield, MO 00000
April 1, 1991

Ms. Martha Wright
Customer Service
Super Sofa
Kansas City, MO 00000

Dear Ms. Wright:

I am writing to complain about your company's two-month delay in delivering my sofa. My order number is 123456.

I ordered a sofa on January 15, 1991. The cost was $350. I was told that the sofa was going to be delivered on February 1, 1991. Last month, I was told it would be delivered by March 15, 1991. It has not yet been delivered, and no one at your company is returning my phone calls.

Please call me at 000-000-0000 to tell me when my sofa will be delivered. If I do not hear from you by April 15, 1991, I will cancel my order and ask for my money to be refunded. Thank you.

Sincerely,

Robert Jones

Letter offering your opinion

200 Palm Circle
Terryton, CA 00000

May 24, 1991

The Editor
The Terryton Times
789 Overland Road
Terryton, CA 00000

Dear Sir or Madam:

I disagree with your editorial of May 22, in which you support higher city taxes. The new taxes that the mayor proposes will hurt working people like me and thousands of others. But they will not affect rich business owners who could afford to pay higher taxes.

Your newspaper is called "The Paper of the People." I hope you will reconsider your editorial stance to reflect that belief.

Sincerely,

Dana Robins

Dana Robins

These are just a few ideas for ways to write business letters. There are many other ways. The important thing is to decide what you want to say, and then say it.

Seven series of good books for all readers:

WRITERS' VOICES
Selections from the works of America's finest and most popular writers, along with background information, maps, and other supplementary materials. Authors include: Kareem Abdul-Jabbar • Maya Angelou • Bill Cosby • Alex Haley • Stephen King • Loretta Lynn • Larry McMurtry • Amy Tan • Anne Tyler • Abigail Van Buren • Alice Walker • Tom Wolfe, and many others.

NEW WRITERS' VOICES
Anthologies and individual narratives by adult learners. A wide range of topics includes home and family, prison life, and meeting challenges. Many titles contain photographs or illustrations.

OURWORLD
Selections from the works of well-known science writers, along with related articles and illustrations. Authors include David Attenborough and Carl Sagan.

FOR YOUR INFORMATION
Clearly written and illustrated works on important self-help topics. Subjects include: Eating Right • Managing Stress • Getting Fit • About AIDS • Getting Good Health Care, among others.

TIMELESS TALES
Classic myths, legends, folk tales, and other stories from around the world, with special illustrations.

SPORTS
Fact-filled books on baseball, football, basketball, and boxing, with lots of action photos. With read-along tapes narrated by Phil Rizzuto, Frank Gifford, Dick Vitale, and Sean O'Grady.

SULLY GOMEZ MYSTERIES
Fast-paced detective series starring Sully Gomez and the streets of Los Angeles.

WRITE FOR OUR FREE COMPLETE CATALOG:

 SIGNAL HILL®

Signal Hill Publications
P.O. Box 131
Syracuse, NY 13210-0131